Brave Wings

Poetry to Lift Your Spirit!

Nitin Jain

BookLeaf Publishing

India | USA | UK

Made with ❤ on the BookLeaf Publishing Platform
www.bookleafpub.in
www.bookleafpub.com

Dedication

This book is dedicated to those who seek wisdom, personal growth, and a deeper understanding of life through the power of poetry. It is for open minds willing to explore new perspectives, eager hearts striving for self-improvement, and those committed to lifelong learning.

Life is a rare and precious journey, filled with both beauty and challenges, and this poem collection serves as a tribute to its resilience, hope, and limitless possibilities.

May these words inspire you to live bravely, embrace change, and discover the strength within to overcome every obstacle on your path.

Preface

Life is a journey filled with challenges, growth, and moments of profound realization. *Brave Wings* is more than just a collection of poems—it is a reflection of resilience, strength, and the unwavering hope that carries us forward. Each poem in this book was born during the most difficult phase of my life, shaped by personal struggles, introspection, and the will to rise above hardships. Over time, I refined these verses, ensuring they hold meaning not just for me but for anyone seeking wisdom, comfort, or motivation. What makes this collection special is its deep connection to everyday life. The themes I have explored—strength in adversity, the pursuit of dreams, self-discovery, and emotional resilience—are universal. Every reader will find a piece of themselves within these pages, as the emotions, experiences, and reflections mirror the struggles and triumphs we all encounter. Through this book, I hope to inspire and uplift, reminding you that even in life's toughest moments, hope and grit will guide the way. Let these poems be a source of strength and a reminder that a thread of hope always remains.

Acknowledgements

First and foremost, I extend my deepest gratitude to my inner self—the quiet voice that encouraged me to introspect, reflect, and pour my thoughts into words. It was in my most challenging moments that I found the strength to write, turning emotions into poetry and struggles into lessons. A heartfelt thank you to my family, whose unwavering support has been my greatest strength. Their belief in me, through every endeavor, has given me the confidence to pursue my passion and share my words with the world. A special thanks to *BookLeaf Publishing* for providing this incredible platform for self-publishing. This opportunity has allowed me to bring my poetic journey to life and share it with readers who resonate with its essence. To everyone who picks up this book, thank you for being part of this journey. May these words inspire, heal, and remind you of the power of hope and resilience. ***Thank you for taking the time to read my book. I would love to hear your thoughts on my poems! Feel free to connect with me on Instagram @nitinjainindia or reach out via email at eboxnitin@yahoo.co.in***

Life Comes Once – Embrace It

In this world that changes fast,
Uncertainty holds us in its grasp.
One great mystery still remains,
Our final breath—none can explain.

Each day we face both stress and fear,
The weight of duties we hold dear.
Expectations rise and climb,
Needs keep growing, time by time.

We wear a smile, yet deep inside,
Sorrows linger, worries hide.
Comparing lives, we lose our way,
Still, somehow, we live the day.

They say a balanced heart and mind,
Brings the joy we seek to find.
But how to reach that peaceful state,
When burdens press with heavy weight?

Some give in to choices wrong,
Some feel they don't belong.
Yet before you lose all hope,
Pause—believe, learn to cope!

Life comes once—no second chance,
A fleeting gift, a sacred dance.
This thought alone can light the way,
And bring us hope for brighter days.

Ease the weight, be kind, be free,
Embrace the joy life lets you see.
Problems won't just fade in one night,
But patience leads to morning light.

Mistakes are made—don't be dismayed,
Learn, improve, don't be afraid.
Seek wisdom, listen to your heart,
Each new dawn's a chance to restart.

Add some laughter, share some cheer,
Let your light shine bright and clear.
Though growth may come a step too slow,
Remember, life's a one-time show.

Meditate, let worries cease,

Bridge the gap from stress to peace.
Live today, embrace the chance,
For life comes once—so let's DANCE!

Life Lesson from this poem :

Life is fleeting and full of uncertainties, but instead of
being weighed down by worries and comparisons,
embrace each moment with patience, kindness, and
resilience. Mistakes are part of growth, and every new
day is a chance to restart. Find balance, seek peace, and
live with joy—because life is a one-time dance.

The Will to Do

Sometimes, we simply have to try,
With no clear path, no reason why.
Knowing nothing—where to start,
Knowing nothing—yet playing our part.

What we are given is just a thought,
A pile of papers, a task unsought.
A command to act, but no clear guide,
Yet still, we march, with strength inside.

What we hold is an ember bright,
An idea burning, a will to fight.
A challenge calling, bold and true,
A test of heart—what will we do?

It's not for pride, nor for show,
Not for the ego, high or low.
It's for the dream, the fire, the way,
The strength to rise, come what may.

Knowing nothing, yet we strive,
Through doubt and dark, we come alive.
Sometimes, we must push on through,
And achieve what none expect us to!

Life Lesson from this poem :
Even when the path is unclear, trust in your inner
strength and take the first step. Growth comes from
pushing forward despite doubts, and true achievement
lies in perseverance. Believe, strive, and you may
accomplish what once seemed impossible.

Shades of Radiance

I once stood in shadows, lost in my own hue,
A canvas of darkness, unsure of my view.
I let the world whisper, "You're less than the rest,"
And carried the weight of its words on my chest.

But time, like a river, began to unfold,
A story of beauty, of courage untold.
I saw in the mirror, not flaws, but a spark,
A light that could glow even in the darkest dark.

I looked all around, and I saw my reflection,
In faces of strength, in every direction.
Dark skin, wheatish tones, a spectrum so wide,
Each one a masterpiece, a source of pride.

We're painted by hands that know no mistake,
A force beyond color, a love that won't break.
It gave me my breath, my dreams, and my fire,
A soul that can rise, a heart that aspires.

No longer confined by the world's narrow sight,
I stand in my truth, I embrace my light.
For brightness isn't borrowed, it comes from within,
A flame that burns steady, through thick and through
thin.

So let them speak words that may dim or divide,
I'll walk with my head high, my spirit as guide.
For I am the artist, the dreamer, the fight,
And I choose to feel radiant, bold, and bright.

Shades of radiance, in every tone,
We are the beauty the world has known.
No matter the color, no matter the skin,
The brightest of lights always shine from within.

Life Lesson from this poem:
True beauty and strength come from within, not from
the world's judgments. Embrace your uniqueness, stand
in your truth, and let your inner light shine—because
confidence and self-acceptance are what truly make you
radiant.

The Last Breath

A mystery vast, a silent thread,
No soul can trace where it has led.

We've touched the stars, we've claimed the deep,
Yet death's own secret, life must keep.

We climb, we build, we chase, we roam,
But none can call this world their home.

For time is swift, like waves that break,
And none can know which breath we take—
Will be the last, the final sigh,
The whisper soft, the last goodbye.

Yet fear it not, this sacred friend,
The gate where all our journeys end.

Embrace it with a heart set free,
For death is not the end, but the key—
A passage into light untold,

Where souls take flight, where hands let go.

So live this day with fearless grace,
Let love and laughter fill this space.

For when the final breath is near,
Let it not find regret or fear.

Let it be proud, let it be pure,
A song of life that shall endure.

For when it comes, stand strong, stand bright,
And walk with peace into the light.

Life Lesson from this poem:
Life is fleeting, and death is not an end but a passage.
Instead of fearing the unknown, embrace each moment
with love, courage, and joy. Live without regret, so when
your final breath comes, it finds you at peace, having
truly lived.

The Power of Music

Music is thunder, bold and bright,
Breaking silence, igniting light.
It moves the soul, it stirs the mind,
A force unchained, unbound by time.

Music can heal, music can fight,
It lifts the fallen, fuels the night.
With every note, a spark is born,
Turning pain to strength reborn.

Music unites, no walls remain,
It speaks in love, beyond all names.
No creed, no color, wealth, or fate—
Music calls, and all relate.

Music is fire, fierce yet kind,
A storm, a whisper, intertwined.
It bends no knee, it fears no chain,
Yet soothes the heart, dissolves all pain.

Let music reign, let echoes swell,
A voice of peace, a battle yell.
For even in the hush so deep,
Music lives—it never sleeps.

Life Lesson from this poem :
Music is a universal force that heals, unites, and inspires.
It transcends barriers, turning pain into strength and
silence into light. Let music fill your soul, for its power
never fades.

A Night of Endless Stars

A million stars may light the sky,
Yet only thousands meet my eye.
And those were mine to freely see,
A universe just meant for me.

The cold breeze whispers, soft and light,
A touch so pure, a breath so bright.
Like heaven's hand upon my skin,
A gentle call, a peace within.

Still I lay upon the ground,
Where silence sings without a sound.
The horizon stretched, the stars grew near,
A boundless world, so calm, so clear.

Like a baby in a mother's keep,
My body rests, my soul sleeps deep.
No sorrow lingers, no weight remains,
Only the night, the stars, the plains.

For never had life shone so bright,
As it did upon that wondrous night.

Life Lesson from this poem :
Peace and wonder are found in life's simplest moments.
When we pause to embrace the beauty around us, we
realize that true joy comes not from having everything,
but from appreciating what is already ours.

The Strength of Patience

Patience is heavier than a mighty stone,
Stronger than an explosion's tone.
It teaches lessons words can't say,
To toil, to learn, to find our way.

Patience guides where knowledge lacks,
It builds resolve, it mends the cracks.
It teaches us to forgive and let go,
To honor the wisdom that others know.

Patience whispers, "Sit and think,"
"Pause and learn, let ideas sync."
Then it urges, "Rise and act,"
With steady hands and a heart intact.

Patience teaches us to smile in pain,
To wait for joys we've yet to gain.
To cherish wins, both big and small,
To brace for what the future calls.

For patience is the silent key,
To better moments yet to be.
It shapes our hours, our nights, our days,
And lights the path in unseen ways.

Life Lesson from this poem:
Patience is the quiet strength that shapes our journey. It teaches us to endure, grow, and trust in the timing of life. With patience, we find wisdom, resilience, and the path to greater things ahead.

The Path to Strength

In life's long journey, we often find,
Tasks unwanted, yet we're confined.
No passion burns, no interest thrives,
Yet we must act—to live, to strive.

A new job starts, a chapter unfolds,
Thrown in waters deep and cold.
Many face this, day by day,
Yet results, not reasons, pave the way.

For once you master the task at hand,
The power to choose is your command.
What seemed a burden, dull and weak,
May shape the strength you one day seek.

Others may see what we do not,
A hidden gift, a skill unthought.
They hand us work we'd cast aside,
Yet through the storm, we stand with pride.

For only trials forge the strong,
And hardships shape where we belong.
A challenge met, a lesson learned,
Respect and wisdom—both are earned.

Each minute holds a chance untold,
A step towards a dream of gold.
Without the trials, the lessons, the pain,
No skill is honed, no heights we gain.

The work we fear is not as tough,
With will and planning, it's enough.
True efforts never go unseen,
They light the path, they build the dream.

But seek not praise with every deed,
For instant reward is a hollow need.
Patience guides the steady climb,
Greatness grows in quiet time.

So take the work, embrace the test,
Strive each day, give it your best.
For he who quits before the fight,
Walks a road with endless night.

Let struggles shape, let lessons teach,
Your destined heights are within reach.

For those who dare, the strong, the rare,
The path to strength is always there.

Life Lesson from this poem:
Embrace challenges, even those you do not choose, for
they shape your strength and open unseen opportunities.
True growth comes from perseverance, and every
struggle is a step toward mastery and success. Stay
patient, work hard, and let your efforts pave the way to
greatness.

If Only Fate Allowed

We are far apart, yet near in heart,
Our feelings stronger than the miles that part.
We talked, we laughed, we shared our days,
Made each other feel cherished in countless ways.

Beauty surrounds me, yet none compare,
For I seek the soul, the love, the care.
And in your heart, so pure, so true,
I found a world that feels like home with you.

I'd rather perish than cause you pain,
Your trust in me won't be in vain.
For in you, I see a woman so rare—
Strong yet gentle, beyond compare.

Grace and wisdom, heart and mind,
A soul so radiant, warm and kind.
A dreamer, a fighter, destined to rise,
A light so bright beneath the skies.

I wish you knew the thoughts I keep,
The prayers I whisper before I sleep.
Two souls longing, yet held apart,
Bound by fate, yet joined in heart.

Perhaps it's God's will - this space, this test,
Yet I pray He rethinks what He deems best.

Life Lesson from this poem:
True connections transcend distance, for love and trust
are not bound by space. When hearts are sincere, even
separation cannot weaken the bond. Faith, patience, and
understanding keep love alive, no matter the miles in
between.

Step by Step, We Rise

Step by step, the path unfolds,
A story of courage, a tale untold.
Not just the peak, nor the prize we chase,
But the lessons we learn in time and space.

The road may twist, the climb feels steep,
Yet hidden in struggle are treasures we keep.
Each little step, each trial we bear,
Shapes who we are with wisdom rare.

If only the end is where we gaze,
The journey itself becomes a maze.
But when we pause, embrace the way,
Every challenge turns to light of day.

Stress and fear may cloud the mind,
If only the finish is what we find.
Yet when we walk with open eyes,
Even failure can make us rise.

For it's not just where we come to stand,
But how we grow, how we expand.
The journey molds, it makes us whole,
More than just a distant goal.

So walk with faith, with heart so wide,
Let passion be your trusted guide.
In each small step, find joy and light,
And the journey itself will shine so bright.

Life Lesson from this poem:
Life is not just about reaching the destination but embracing the journey. Every challenge, step, and setback shapes us, offering wisdom and growth. When we walk with an open heart, even struggles can shine with purpose.

The Power of "No"

A simple word, yet hard to say,
A test of strength along the way.
To tell yourself, "No, not today,"
Takes discipline that won't decay.

For some, it's wrapped in fear and doubt,
Afraid to stand, to speak, to shout.
They chase what's easy, flee the fight,
Yet lose themselves in borrowed light.

Temptations call, they pull, they sway,
The lazy heart drifts far away.
Without a line, without a stand,
They trade their dreams for fleeting sand.

But those who rise, who dare to fight,
Who walk with honor, chase the right.
They stand with courage, firm and tall,
And say "No" when weakness calls.

For strength is found in what we choose,
Not in the things we're scared to lose.
A "No" today, so bold, so wise,
Can lead to where true greatness lies.

Life Lesson from this poem:
True strength lies in the power to say "No"—to
distractions, temptations, and fleeting desires. Discipline
and courage shape our path, and the choices we make
today determine the greatness we achieve tomorrow.

She is the Fire, She is the Storm

She is not a whisper, soft and weak,
She is the thunder when she speaks.
Not an object, not a prize,
She is the sun in her own skies.

They try to write her, line by line,
Yet she is poetry, bold, divine.
Not a chapter in someone's tale,
But the author who will not fail.

She loves with fire, deep and true,
Yet knows love must give back too.
Not a sacrifice, not a test,
She deserves a love that gives its best.

She won't undress to prove her soul,
Her worth is more than body's role.
She won't abandon dreams so bright,
For someone else to steal her light.

Her kindness shines, yet not in vain,
She won't bear burdens laced with pain.
She stands for others, but even more,
She guards her heart, her inner core.

Her dignity, a crown she wears,
Not for sale, nor placed in snares.
Her mind, her sword, so sharp, so wise,
Cuts through deceit, through hidden lies.

She is not just a fleeting part,
She is the world, its beating heart.
A force of nature, bold, untamed,
A story waiting to be named.

Life Lesson from this poem:
Embrace your strength, dignity, and self-worth
unapologetically. You are not defined by how others
perceive you or the roles they try to assign. Like thunder,
let your voice be heard; like the sun, shine in your own
sky. Love deeply but never at the cost of your own light.
Stand strong in your dreams, guard your heart, and
remember—your story is yours to write.

The Gift of Time

Time is a treasure, precious and rare,
A gift so priceless, beyond compare.
Each moment whispers, a chance so bright,
To chase our dreams, to rise, take flight.

The young may think it flows with ease,
Like endless waves upon the seas.
Yet one day, they will pause and see,
How fast it fades, how swift it flees.

A second lost, a breath untold,
A story waiting to unfold.
Wasted hours turn to regret,
Lessons learned but never met.

But time is kind, it gives us space,
To change, to grow, to find our place.
With careful hands and mindful heart,
We shape our fate, we play our part.

So value time, let none be lost,
For every dream, it pays the cost.
Respect its magic, heed its call,
And watch it lead you to stand tall.

Life Lesson from this poem:
Time is the most valuable gift we possess, flowing swiftly
and never returning. While youth may take it for
granted, wisdom reveals its fleeting nature. Every
moment holds the power to shape our future—wasted
time leads to regret, but mindful use opens the door to
growth and success. Cherish time, use it wisely, and it
will guide you toward your dreams.

A Father's Silent Strength

He walks through storms with steady feet,
A heart so strong, yet kind and sweet.
The world may bend, the skies may fall,
But he stands tall, through it all.

He speaks in actions, not in words,
His love is felt but seldom heard.
No crown he wears, no cape in sight,
Yet he's the hero in the night.

He hides his pain behind a smile,
Endures the weight, walks every mile.
At work, he fights, at home, he shields,
His love's the force that never yields.

His hands may roughen, his hair may gray,
But love within won't fade away.
A hug from his son, a kiss from his girl,
To him, these moments are his world.

He asks for nothing, just respect,
A heart so pure, yet oft neglect.
Through all his scars, through all his strife,
A father's love—his greatest life.

Life Lesson from this poem:
True strength is not measured by words or appearances
but by unwavering love, quiet sacrifices, and steadfast
resilience. A father's love may often go unnoticed, yet it
is the foundation upon which families stand. Respect and
cherish those who give selflessly, for their love is the
silent force that shapes our world.

The Power of Three Simple Words

In a world so fast, where time just flies,
We pass each other with distant eyes.

We smile, we nod, and walk away,
Yet someone's heart may beg to say—
"I'm hurting, lost, unseen, unheard,"
But no one stops to share a word.

A simple phrase, so small, so true,
Could paint their sky a brighter hue.
"How are you?"—just **three words** long,
Yet they can heal, make spirits strong.

A quiet soul, a hidden tear,
May find some hope when you are near.
The friend who laughs, the one who stays,
Might be lost in silent days.

The stranger standing all alone,

Might need to hear a softer tone.
We never know what one might bear,
A heart weighed down with deep despair.

But kindness whispered, warm and true,
Can change a life—because of you.
So ask with love, and truly see,
The power in this question free.

A world less lonely, bright and new,
Begins when we ask, "How are you?"

Life Lesson from this poem:
In the rush of life, we often overlook the silent struggles
of others. A simple act of kindness, like genuinely
asking, *"How are you?"*, can bring light to someone's
darkest moments. True connection lies in small gestures
of care, and by taking the time to truly see and listen, we
can make the world a little less lonely and a lot more
compassionate.

The Strength of Being Sensitive

In a world so loud, so tough, so fast,
Some hearts feel deeply, make love last.
A sensitive soul, so pure, so true,
Sees the world in a kinder view.

Being sensitive isn't weak,
It shows the strength that others seek.
To care, to love, to truly feel,
Takes courage, faith, and heart so real.

They do not shout, they do not fight,
Yet stand for truth with quiet might.
No need to judge, no need to blame,
They shine with kindness, not with fame.

So wear your heart upon your sleeve,
Give, forgive, and always believe.
For in this life, the greatest part—
Is a sensitive yet fearless heart.

In a world that often values toughness over tenderness, true strength lies in sensitivity. Being kind, compassionate, and deeply feeling is not a weakness—it is a rare courage that brings light to others. A fearless heart does not seek validation through noise or power but stands firm in love, truth, and grace. Embrace your sensitivity, for it is the quiet force that makes life richer and more meaningful.

Rise Again

When the world feels dark, and hope seems gone,
When every road feels rough and long,
When pain and sorrow weigh you down,
And silence echoes—no joyful sound.

When you're lost, frustrated, drowning in pain,
When love feels distant, and tears fall like rain,
When humiliation, torture, and loss take hold,
And the fire within you feels so cold.

But why surrender? Why let go?
Why let despair steal your soul?
Life's not meant to end this way,
For storms will pass, the night turns day.

Death is nature's silent call,
Not for the weak, not yours at all.
Your strength, your fire, still remain,
Rise once more, break every chain.

If you can give up, then why not fight?
Why not chase the morning light?
If nothing matters anymore,
Then live with courage—fear no more.

Laugh louder, breathe deeper, dance in the rain,
Turn sorrow to wisdom, transform your pain.
Suicide's a whisper, a shadow, a test,
But life is the answer—so live it your best.

Restart, rebuild, open your heart,
Let go of the past, embrace a new start.
For you are more than your darkest days,
A soul meant to shine in endless ways.

So rise again, stand tall, be free,
The world awaits your destiny.

Life Lesson from this poem:
No matter how dark and painful life may seem, storms
will always pass, and new beginnings are possible.
Strength lies in rising again, embracing challenges, and
choosing to live with courage. Instead of surrendering to
despair, transform your struggles into wisdom, seek joy
in the little moments, and realize that you are meant for
greatness. Life is a journey of resilience—so stand tall,
break free, and shine.

The Weight of Anger

Anger is a shadow, dark and deep,
A restless force that steals our sleep.
It claws and gnaws, it twists and binds,
A poison seeping through our minds.

It clouds the mind, it blinds the soul,
A fire that rages beyond control.
It pushes love and kindness away,
Leaving only shadows in its fray.

"I am right," the angry claim,
Yet righteousness is not their aim.
For wisdom speaks in tones so calm,
A healing touch, a soothing balm.

True strength is not in rage displayed,
But in the patience wisdom made.
To understand, to empathize,
To see the world through clearer eyes.

Anger springs from pride and fear,
From bias, ignorance, and sneers.
It thrives where empathy is thin,
A battle fought from deep within.

Yet there's a time when anger's flame
May rise to shield, to guard, to claim.
When safety's threatened, lives at stake,
It stands as armor, no mistake.

But in the quiet, in the still,
The strongest hearts bend to their will.
They choose the path of peace and grace,
A steady hand, a gentle face.

For anger's power, though it may seem,
Is but a fleeting, hollow dream.
True strength is found in self-control,
In mastering the tempest of the soul.

So let us seek the wiser way,
To face the trials of each day.
With patience, love, and hearts sincere,
We'll conquer anger, year by year.

Life Lesson from this poem:
True strength lies not in anger but in patience,
understanding, and self-control. While anger may feel
justified, it clouds judgment and pushes away kindness.
Wisdom speaks in calmness, and those who master their
emotions find peace and deeper connections. Choose
empathy over rage, for true power comes from self-
discipline and compassion.

The Phone's Grip, Life's Slip!

The smartphone glows, it calls my name,
A world of pleasure, a tempting game.
With every swipe, the minutes fly,
Yet real life passes right outside.

A hundred reasons to stare and scroll,
But dreams and goals pay the toll.
A message dings, my time it takes,
While love and laughter slip away.

My health declines, my mind grows weak,
I chase a world that's cold and bleak.
Family waits, but I don't see,
Their moments lost because of me.

Work undone, my passion fades,
Trapped inside this endless maze.
The world outside, so fresh, so bright,
Yet here I sit, lost in the light.

What if I choose to break these chains?
To live, to love, to dream again?
To walk, to talk, to touch, to feel,
To make my moments true and real.

A phone's a tool, not life itself,
It must not steal my time and health.
I choose to use it **wise and well,**
Not let it cast a numbing spell.

So lift your eyes, go seize the day,
Don't let your life just drift away.
For time is gold, don't let it flee,
Live your life **smart and free.**

Life lesson from this poem :

Smartphones are powerful but can become a silent thief
of time, health, and relationships. While they offer
endless distractions, real happiness comes from living in
the moment, nurturing passions, and connecting with
loved ones. Use your phone wisely—let it be a tool for
growth, not a barrier to life. Time is precious—live smart
and free.

The Power of Practice

Your mind is a garden, where thoughts will grow,
What you plant and nurture will start to show.
If fed with doubt, fear, and despair,
Negativity lingers in the air.

But just like muscles trained each day,
Your thoughts can also shape the way.
What you repeat will soon take hold,
A habit formed, a story told.

Think in darkness, the world seems gray,
Train for light, and you'll find the way.
See a struggle or see a chance,
It's all a matter of how you glance.

To break the chains of thoughts unkind,
Practice hope and free your mind.
At first, it's hard, it takes some fight,
But step by step, you'll see the light.

Choose to see the good, the bright,
Turn your storms into guiding light.
For what you think, you soon become,
So shape your mind—your time has come!

Life Lesson from this poem:
Our thoughts shape our reality. Just as practice makes perfect, the way we think—whether positive or negative—becomes a habit that influences our lives. If we constantly dwell on negativity, we train our minds to see obstacles instead of opportunities. However, by consciously practicing positive thinking, we can rewire our mindset to focus on growth, resilience, and solutions. The key lesson is that we have the power to shape our thoughts, and in doing so, we shape our destiny. Train your mind to see the good, and life will respond in kind.

The Gift of Laughter

In a world so fast, where worries grow,
A simple smile can steal the show.
A burst of laughter, pure and bright,
Can turn the dark into the light.

It dances soft upon the air,
A melody beyond compare.
It lifts the heart, it soothes the soul,
It makes the broken pieces whole.

Through every trial, pain, or tear,
Laughter whispers, "Hope is near."
It binds us close, both friend and kin,
A spark of joy that dwells within.

So laugh today, let burdens fade,
Find joy in moments softly made.
For in this life, both wild and free,
Laughter is love's sweet melody.

Laughter is a powerful healer that lightens burdens, strengthens relationships, and reminds us that joy can be found even in difficult times. It teaches us to embrace simple moments, cherish connections, and find hope even in darkness. By allowing ourselves to laugh, we invite happiness, ease stress, and make life's journey more beautiful. In the end, laughter is not just an emotion—it's a lesson in resilience, love, and the art of truly living.